Contents

I like **cheese**.

Do you like cheese?

There are many different kinds of cheese.

Good Food

I Like Cheese

By Robin Pickering

Children's Press
A Division of Grolier Publishing
New York / London / Hong Kong / Sydney
Danbury, Connecticut

Photo Credits: Cover, p. 5, 7, 9, 11, 13, 15, 17, 19, 21a, 21b, 21c by Thaddeus Harden; 21d © Comstock

Contributing Editor: Jennifer Ceaser
Book Design: Michael DeLisio

Library of Congress Cataloging-in-Publication Data

Pickering, Robin.
  I like cheese / by Robin Pickering.
    p. cm. – (Good food)
  Includes bibliographical references and index.
  Summary: Describes different kinds of cheese and how they may be eaten.
  ISBN 0-516-23082-4 (lib. bdg.) – ISBN 0-516-23007-7 (pbk.)
  1. Cheese—Juvenile literature. 2. Cookery (Cheese)—Juvenile literature. [1.Cheese.] I.
  Title.
TX382.P53 2000
  641.6'73—dc21   00-024372

5

I like yellow cheese.

This cheese is **chewy**.

I eat the cheese on bread.

I like **gooey** cheese.

It's fun to eat!

9

I like **chunks** of white cheese.

I put the cheese on salad.

11

This cheese looks like **powder**.

I shake it on pizza.

I like cheese with holes.

The holes are called eyes.

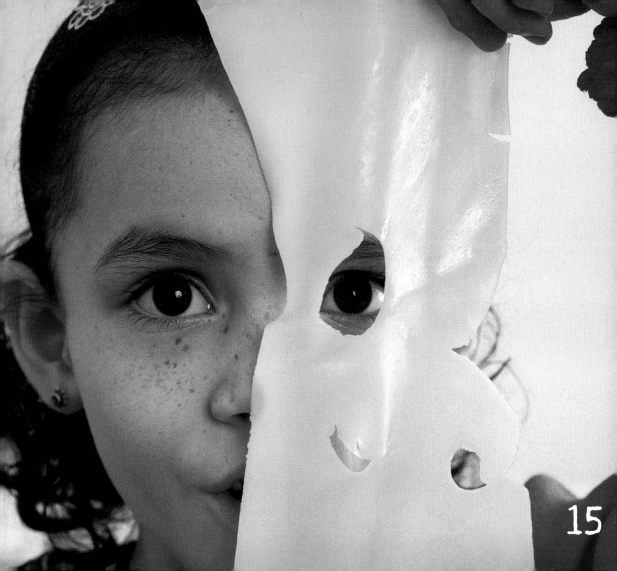

My mom likes **stinky**, yucky cheese.

I think it smells like dirty socks!

I like **melted** cheese.

It's very hot.

I like to dip chips into the cheese.

Which kind of cheese do you like to eat?

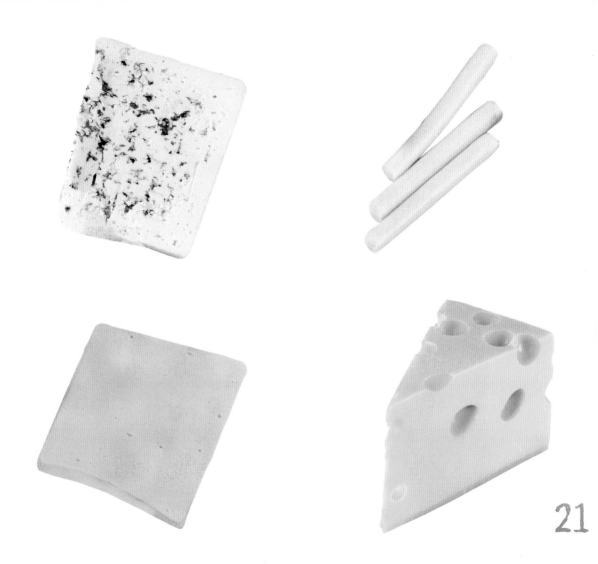

21

New Words

cheese (**cheez**) a food made from the milk of certain animals

chewy (**chu**-ee) something that has to be chewed a lot

chunks (**chungkz**) thick pieces

gooey (**gu**-ee) soft and sticky

melted (**melt**-ed) something that is heated until it loses its shape

powder (**pow**-der) tiny bits of things that are ground up

stinky (**stink**-ee) smells very bad

To Find Out More

Books

Extra Cheese, Please!: Mozzarella's Journey from Cow to Pizza
by Cris Peterson
Boyds Mills Press

Kids' First Cookbook
by The American Cancer Society
American Cancer Society

More Cheese, Please!: A Book About Trying New Foods
by Joshua Morris and Sue Kueffner
Reader's Digest

Web Sites

Cheese.com—All About Cheese!
http://www.cheese.com
This site shows different kinds of cheese and talks about where they come from.

I Love Cheese
http://www.ilovecheese.com
Information about cheese, including the history of cheese.
Check out the foods you can make with cheese!

Index

About the Author
Robin Pickering is a writer, editor, and yoga instructor living in Brooklyn, New York.

Reading Consultants

Kris Flynn, Coordinator, Small School District Literacy, The San Diego County Office of Education

Shelly Forys, Certified Reading Recovery Specialist, W.J. Zahnow Elementary School, Waterloo, IL

Peggy McNamara, Professor, Bank Street College of Education, Reading and Literacy Program